GRANDFATHER'S HANDBOOK

HOW TO UNDERSTAND AND HAVE FUN WITH YOUR GRANDCHILD

To My Bro Bob

By
John Dunzer

5/6/2000

Great Times Press, Lake Arrowhead, California

GRANDFATHER'S HANDBOOK

HOW TO UNDERSTAND AND HAVE FUN WITH YOUR GRANDCHILD

BY JOHN DUNZER

Published by:

Great Times Press
Post Office Box 378
Lake Arrowhead, CA, 92352

Copyright© 1995 by John Dunzer
First Printing 1995
Printed in the United States of America

Library of Congress Card Number: 95-94339
Dunzer, John
   Grandfather's Handbook: How to understand and have fun with your Grandchild / by John Dunzer, - 1st ed.
        p. cm.
Includes bibliographical references and index
ISBN: 0-9646178-9-7 $12.95 (pbk)
1. Grandparent and Child   I. Title
2. Intergenerational relations
HQ759.9.D92   1995
306.874'5--dc20

DEDICATION

"TO THE MILLIONS WHO ARE MAKING AN EFFORT

TO IMPROVE THE LIVES OF OUR

CHILDREN AND GRANDCHILDREN,

I DEDICATE THIS BOOK"

Table of Contents

Table of Contents

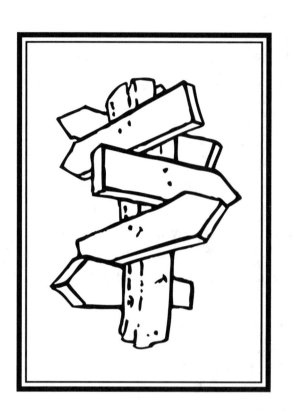

INTRODUCTION

A Roadmap

WHY DOES THE WORLD NEED A GRANDFATHER BOOK?

There are 25 million Grandfathers in the United States. This is about 10% of the country's 1995 population. One in three adult males are Grandfathers. Across the world there are hundreds of millions of Grandfathers. Males assume many roles throughout their lifetime; father, husband, student, worker, citizen, friend, neighbor, etc. Most of us can also look forward to becoming a Grandfather.

This is a role which can occupy us actively for several decades as our Grandchildren move from infancy to adulthood.

Research has shown that, on an average, we do not do a good job as Grandfathers. About 20% of us have little or no contact with our Grandchildren. A large percentage of us still consider active Grandparenthood to be a task for Grandmothers. When we do take an active interest, we are involved primarily with our Grandsons when they are young children. We neglect all our Grandchildren when they are infants and during their difficult teen years.

We sit and bemoan the state of the world and our Country and note the sorry state of families today. Yet, when it comes to making a meaningful effort with our own flesh and blood, we look for someone else to do it for us. To top it all off, we give lip service to the practice of active Grandfatherhood when this is the opportunity for each of us to have the MOST FUN OF OUR LIVES.

During the last few months, I have read over 20 books on Grandparenting. There were books by medical doctors, child psychologists, theologians, and by caring Grandmothers. Grandfathers are described as assistants, at best, and uninvolved, at worst, in today's Grandparenting.

Much has been made recently of the difference in communication styles between males and females (i.e."Men are from Mars and Women are from Venus"). As males, Grandfathers tend to want to identify and solve problems rather than discussing problems as Grandmothers might wish to do. Communicating with Grandfathers is different than communicating with Grandmothers.

I concluded that the WORLD DOES NOT NEED A TEXTBOOK ABOUT GRANDFATHERING. Most males are simply not going to read a textbook on being a Grandfather. Typically these books are filled with story after story and example after example. Most of us are not going to be child development specialists. If we have an interest in being a Grandfather, what we want is a roadmap; a program, a solution. This HANDBOOK IS A ROADMAP; a roadmap to make the role of Grandfather rewarding and fun for Grandfathers and our Grandchildren.

Grandmothers are most welcome, but they have much more experience in their Grandparenting role than we Grandfathers. This handbook may not meet their needs. It is organized as a series of questions and answers that a Grandfather might ask before becoming committed to taking seriously the role of Grandfather. Hopefully, the wording of these questions will evoke a chuckle along the way.

WHAT'S IN THIS HANDBOOK ANYWAY?

What exactly does "Grandfather's Handbook" contain that could possibly interest us? The handbook is made up of three parts:

Part One - Understanding Each Other
Part Two - Having Fun Together
Part Three - Dealing With Problems

Part One, "Understanding Each Other", consists of four chapters which address the major issues of the Grandfather/Grandchild relationship.

- Chapter 1 - "The Grandfather" talks about our favorite person, ourself, and what WE CAN GAIN from active Grandfatherhood.
- Chapter 2 - "The Grandchild" starts with a discussion of whether Grandfathers are really needed and identifies what we, as Grandfathers, MUST BE PREPARED TO DO if this is to be a worthwhile experience for us and our Grandchild.

- Chapter 3 - " The Rest of the Cast" answers
                questions on how we need to pro-
                ceed with Grandmother, the par-
                ents and other Grandparents if we
                are going to STAY OUT OF HOT
                WATER.
- Chapter 4 - " Making the Connection " suggests
                ways to get the BIGGEST BANG
                (most rewards) FOR THE INVEST-
                MENT (our time and money)

Part Two, "Having Fun Together", consists of five
chapters describing an action program for the time
we spend with our Grandchild.
- Chapter 5 - "Teaching a Grandchild" catalogs
                our skills in eleven areas and
                MATCHES THESE SKILLS WITH
                THE INTERESTS of our
                Grandchild.
- Chapter 6 - "Grandchild Activities" recom-
                mends a wide range of in-house
                and community ACTIVITIES THAT
                WILL INTEREST our Grandchild.
- Chapter 7 - "Traveling with a Grandchild" sug-
                gests a wide SPECTRUM OF TRIP
                IDEAS for Grandfather and
                Grandchild.

- Chapter 8 - "Family Ties" discusses Grandfather's role in PROVIDING A FAMILY HISTORY for our Grandchild.
- Chapter 9 - "Planning For Success" identifies the method each of us can use to develop a GRANDFATHER PLAN TO MAXIMIZE THE FUN we have with our Grandchild.

Part Three, "Dealing With Problems", consists of two chapters which introduce a number of problems we may encounter in our role as Grandfather and suggests ways to deal with them.

- Chapter 10 - " We Live Too Far Away " suggests creative ways that Grandfather can SOLVE THE DISTANCE PROBLEM, one of today's challenges of Grandfatherhood.
- Chapter 11 - " Ups and Downs " discusses today's social environment and how Grandfathers can CONTRIBUTE TO THEIR GRANDCHILD'S WELL BEING.

EPILOGUE - Provides an answer to my seven year old Grandson's question, "Grandpa, why isn't everyone HAVING THIS MUCH FUN ?"

Want a shortcut? Go directly to Part Two, "Having Fun Together". Unfortunately, most of us need more of a framework for success which the other parts of the Handbook provide. The Appendix provides a list of Organizations that can help deal with a wide range of family problems. The Appendix also contains a Bibliography and an Index.

PART ONE

Understanding Each Other

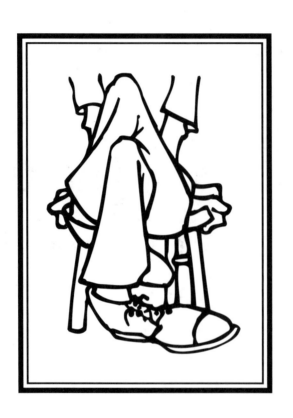

CHAPTER 1

The Grandfather

WHAT'S SO SPECIAL ABOUT BEING A GRANDFATHER?

Historically Grandfathers have been important. In the past, they held the store of knowledge and experience that enabled survival. Respect for elders in the American culture has declined in recent times as basic survival skills have become less important. We became a culture that worshiped youth. Elders, including Grandfathers, were put on the shelf.

We no longer shared the homes, communities, or the lives of our children and grandchildren. We all went our own ways and being a Grandfather appeared to become unimportant as did the entire concept of an extended family.

The pendulum is swinging back with the rise in interest by our society in "traditional values". With the family being under attack from all sides, it appears now that many of us are rethinking our role in the family. Most of us have fond memories of the great joy that we experienced when we were active participants in a family. Today the term family may not mean the nuclear family but it does mean gatherings of both the old and young who share common bonds.

Grandfathers have always had a deep interest in Grandchildren because it was up to us to ensure that the next generations would survive. Grandchildren are the future for a Grandfather; there is the knowledge that the family will go on. Grandfatherhood is our opportunity to present the values around which we live our lives and to pass along the skills that we have acquired.

Parents and Grandparents share these interests in the Grandchild but as a Grandfather we are able to utilize quite a different approach than Parents. This is what makes being a Grandfather so special and potentially so much fun. Being a Grandfather is unique because our relationship to the child is not overwhelmed by the day-to-day details of living that diverted our attention when we were Fathers. It's not up to us to teach them everything they need to know; to take the full responsibility for raising them. Parents must dispense affection based on the child's conformance to their rules. Grandfathers can offer affection and friendship with few strings attached.

There is much less potential for conflict between us and our Grandchildren than there was, as we probably remember too well, when we were Fathers. This doesn't mean that we should eliminate all discipline and let the Grandchildren run wild with no rules or boundaries but it does mean that wherever possible we should "cut them a little slack on the small stuff". Is this fair? Probably not, but part of our function is to serve as one of the few adults who can provide sanctuary. A wise friend who can help these children sort out the problems that are a part of growing up.

This unique friendship with a child is a great chance for us to rekindle our spirit of play; to rediscover the spirit of adventure and discovery from our youth. We can share our skills, knowledge, and experience with someone who really matters. Someone who is connected to us by both biology and kinship.

As a Grandfather, we know that we have something to do that is truly important. It is another tool that we can use to make these years the best time of our lives. An opportunity provided to us because we are Grandfathers.

WHEN DID I GET OLD ENOUGH TO BE A GRANDFATHER?

It is a contradiction to be young and a Grandfather. While some of us become Grandfathers before we are forty and others after sixty or later, when we realize that we are Grandfathers most of us feel that the clock has passed high noon and that we are in the afternoon of life.

We might pride ourselves on being more youthful than most Grandfathers. That being a Grandfather doesn't necessarily mean that we are old. It does say that time is passing for us. To have a Grandchild says all of a sudden that we have moved up a whole generation. No one asked our permission to make us a Grandfather; there is nothing we can do. Don't get too discouraged however because as a group we are healthier and much more active than Grandfathers

in the past. We are the first generation of
Grandfathers that can look forward to about 20
more years of active life than our own Grandfathers.
Many of us at 65 will be seeing our Grandchildren
into their high school years yet we can expect an
average of 15 more years of a healthy, active life.

Just because we are still very active physically
doesn't mean that we are not undergoing big
changes in our lives. Many of us are finding it easier to relax. We are no longer so competitive or com-
pulsive. Our once dominant concerns with work are
changing. We feel a great intensity about those
things we do consider important and are becoming
much more interested in people and relationships.

We spend time separating out the things that
are really important to us and reach for whatever
we have missed along the way. Many experience for
the first time, after a lifetime of raising our own
children, that we have some discretionary income.
Most of us are just as involved in life and work as
our children. Retirement is something to be considered in the distant future, if at all.

Being a Grandfather certainly doesn't mean
packing in our former life and settling down to our
declining years. What it means is that we have
another of life's opportunities to expand ourselves
and to add another identity, being a Grandfather.

WILL BEING A GRANDFATHER INTERFERE WITH MY GOLF GAME?

There was a time when a Grandfather didn't have to do anything special to enjoy the respect and love of our Grandchildren, just being an elder was enough. Today we've got to work for this respect. This takes effort and time. Being a Grandfather could and should be a lot more rewarding and enriching than it is for most Grandfathers. We will have a better time if we learn a little more about how to go about it. We need to learn to understand:
- ourselves as potential Grandfathers
- our Grandchildren as they grow and change
- the other adults in our Grandchildren's lives
- how the Grandparent/Grandchild relationship can be established and maintained
- how to make the most out of the time we get to spend with our Grandchildren
- how to deal with some problems likely to occur

If we as Grandfathers are going to spend about 30 years of our lives in this role, we would be silly not to want to maximize the benefits of this relationship to ourselves and our Grandchildren. Learning a little bit about being a Grandfather is likely to take the time it takes to play about nine holes. Actually being a Grandfather to our Grandchildren will take much more time. But I guarantee that when we hear our Grandchild tell someone that "my Grandfather is the best in the whole world", we will experience a thrill unmatched by winning any grand slam tournament.

CAN'T I JUST DO WHAT COMES NATURALLY?

Children are not like they were when we were raising our family. They are much more sophisticated and aware of the world and what is going on around them. Families are much different also. Fathers and Mothers may have much different roles in raising their children. Divorce and alternatives to the nuclear family are now the rule rather than the exception. We may not like this but this is the reality of our Grandchild's world. The old model we have in mind of how a Grandfather, a Parent, and a Grandchild interrelate and behave probably does not fit the world in which we are now living. During our lifetime Grandfathering has become increasingly complicated.

On a more positive note, Grandfathers are no longer relegated to a rocking chair approach to their Grandchildren. We are more knowledgeable, more fit and better off financially than our predecessors. We have better transportation systems and communication tools to bridge the distances to our Grandchildren. There are also fewer obstacles to males, including Grandfathers, becoming actively involved in the raising of children. Today most of us appreciate that Grandfathers do have the ability to provide a nurturing role within the family and to accept this as a part of our responsibility. Yes, Grandfathers have many natural abilities to successfully interact with their Grandchildren. If we're to make a real impact, we must make the effort to understand the revolution in our family structure.

WHAT'S IN THIS FOR ME ?

So our projected life span is 20 years longer than our Grandfathers; what are we going to do with it? Surely you don't think we should go out to pasture just when we are reaching the peak of our knowledge and experience? We all know that the World is always ready to write us off as insignificant if we let them. Why not use at least a part of this time that we have been given to pass some of our wisdom and values along to our Grandchildren.

We should look at Grandfatherhood as another of life's opportunities to be useful. There is no greater reward for a man than to know that what he is doing is important and is making a difference. Of course, we have worked hard all our lives and are probably still working. We deserve a break, but there are still the tasks and rewards of Grandfatherhood ahead.

We may think that being a Grandfather is just like being a Father except we don't have the energy that we had when we were younger. Nothing could be further from the truth. For example, we might find that we enjoy our Grandchildren more than we did our own children. We're not responsible for these children, their parents are. Relax, we're here to have FUN with them and to enjoy a close, warm, relationship with a child whose happy future means a lot to us. As a Parent we were all wrapped up with training and rules and authority. As a Grandfather, first we get to love them. Sure there are rules but this is primarily a fun experience.

What we need to do is put on our play togs and get down and mix it up with these youngsters. So if we're this fun friend, what are we going to accomplish with these children? Well we're going to be one of their teachers but we get to pick only the sub-jects that interest both of us. We are going to encourage them to explore the roots of their family. Not just our history but also our family's history. We want them to not only feel a part of the past and the present but also see a place for themselves in the future.

We are going to try to serve as a role model, as hard as that might seem. The "Book of Virtues" will be nothing compared to what we will demonstrate to them about courage, compassion, commitment, and community, right? Remember that all this teaching is not a one-way street. Our Grandchild will soon introduce us to his world and a future we may not fully grasp.

What this all adds up to is that the role of Grandfather can measurably add to our reason for living. It can give us the energy, joy and enthusiasm for growth that we may have thought were long gone. IT'S NOT A DUTY, IT'S A PLEASURE.

CHAPTER 2

The Grandchild

DOES A CHILD REALLY NEED A GRANDFATHER?

There are many answers to this rather

simple question. Many males are shaken when they

read in the headlines of today's newspapers and

periodicals "Does a Child Really Need a Father?".

When it comes right down to it, do any of us need

someone who makes zero contribution to our

future? Whether the person being discussed is a

Mother, Father, Husband, Wife, Grandmother or

Grandfather, the answer is "no".

All of us do need those who care about us and
who support us. A better way to ask this question
is to ask the child, "Would you rather have a
Grandfather or would you rather not"? The answer
we get will be an emphatic "I want Grandfathers"
just like it would be if we asked them about a
Mother or Father or Grandmothers. The Grandchild,
the real person of interest here, really wants
Grandfathers. What anybody else thinks, including
Dan Quayle, or Murphy Brown is immaterial.

It is important to develop this basic want into a
relationship where the Grandchild will say, "I need
you". But if the child has wonderful Parents and a
secure and supportive family structure, why does he
need a Grandfather?

This is what a Grandfather can bring to
the table:
- first and foremost, the child must sense that
  we are committed to his or her welfare over
  the long run. Without dependable love there is
  no real relationship.
- specifically what a Grandfather may contribute are:
  • the teaching of:
    - skills that make life interesting

- values that are essential to the growth of the Grandchild as a worthwhile adult.
- family roots and memories to give the Grandchild a sense of place in the world.
• opportunities for the Grandchild to experience fun and fantasy with an adult.
• encouragement to explore the untried
• an understanding and nonjudgmental listener and a potential source of advice (i.e. a wise and trusted counselor)

Most people still choose to believe that Grandfathers enjoy a free ride; playing with the Grandchildren and having fun but, when the going gets tough, turning them over to Grandmother or the Parents. This may be true during a Grandchild's infancy but, soon thereafter, anything meaningful involves us in more than fun and games.

It's demeaning to think of a Grandfather as a mere fairweather friend. Grandchildren appreciate us more if they can talk about their problems with us. We feel more loving and proud when we know they consider us a source of advice.

WHY DOES THIS CHILD KEEP CHANGING?

Children do not mature smoothly but in stages. As Grandfathers, we will be much better equipped to help and communicate with our Grandchildren if we have a basic idea of what this development cycle is all about.

The primary goal of infancy is to make the infant secure in a safe, warm and loving environment. Infants need to be held, caressed, and kissed by happy, caring adults; parents, grandparents, and other responsible caregivers. Some Grandfathers have a problem relating to infants coming from family backgrounds where child raising was a role for women. We should make every effort to attend the birth; it is a powerful experience when a Grandchild comes into the world. Holding this extension of ourselves these first few hours creates an unmatched beginning for our lifetime relationship.

The toddler period is usually defined as starting at the onset of crawling until the child is about two. Our Grandchild is trying to learn selfconfidence, how to use muscles, toilet training, and is introduced to rules. Grandfathers can participate a lot in expanding the Grandchild's world by reading

picture books and introducing new words and experiences. Outdoor climbing and sandbox equipment
will help teach muscle use. We must provide a safe,
childproof environment because our Grandchild will
be into everything at this stage and we want to
avoid saying no-no continually.

Between 2 and 3, known by many as the terrible
twos, our Grandchild wants to establish self-identi-
ty. It is the transition between babyhood and childhood marked by outbursts of tears, temper
tantrums, violent emotions and a lot of demands.
Grandfathers and Grandchildren can have fun if
they do things that won't be frustrating and don't
have a lot of rules. Go to playgrounds and work
together with Play—dough and crayons.

The early childhood years, from 3 to 5, are a
wonderful time for Grandfathers. Grandchildren are
getting ready to venture outside the home. There
are many tasks to master and Grandfathers can
help them try out a whole range of new activities.
Grandchildren are very interested in doing things
with us and can even visit us. They love to play
games and read with us and will speak their
thoughts and feelings freely.

During middle childhood, from 6 to 11, our
Grandchild lives in three different worlds; school,
peers, and family. At school, unlike the family,

acceptance of our Grandchildren is conditional, based on mastery and avoiding inadequacy. Grandfathers can help by finding and developing a special skill with our Grandchild, teaching sports, and helping them develop a love of reading. With peers, our Grandchild develops socialization skills. Invite their friends along on activities like camping trips. Concentrate, during these years on developing a strong one-on-one relationship. Do only things together that we both enjoy; they can sense if we're really not interested in an activity. Possible joint activities include sporting events, hiking and camping, weekend trips, movies, and restaurants, see Chapter 6.

Preadolescence, between age eleven and thirteen, can be a difficult time. Our Grandchildren are trying to destroy their childhood identity and are rebelling against all of adult society. They challenge and criticize everything, including their Parents and Grandparents. We should try not to take this personally. Show them that we understand their quest for independence. We should just do things together that we both enjoy and don't sweat the small stuff. Grandfathers are not required to reform our Grandchildren.

During Adolescence our Grandchildren are trying
to form a new identity separate from their Parents.
We should avoid lecturing our Grandchildren.
Instead seek to become a sounding board. Hopefully,
they will talk to us when they can't talk to their
Parents and in this way we can help them in sort-
ing out their feelings. Offer support and understanding and share with them an excitement about
the world and the future. Try to continue to share
hobbies and skills but many will prefer to be with
their own friends. Despite the problems and stresses,
this can be a wondrous time for Grandfathers. We
should help our Grandchildren find their way and
be there to pick them up when they stumble. This
is a time when Grandfathers can truly shine and be
the major players in pulling the generations back
together after the explosions of Adolescence.

HOW CAN THIS CHILD AND I EVER COMMUNICATE ?

The big age difference between a Grandfather
and his Grandchildren can create many rough
spots. We live in two different worlds. To build
closeness, it is necessary to have some commonality
of our worlds. The only way to do this is for the
Grandfather, with his adult skills, to make the effort

to familiarize himself with the Grandchild's world. LISTEN to what they are saying. We may be the only adults who really listen to them. Try to understand what they are feeling and thinking. Know what they like to do and have a clear picture of the individuality of each Grandchild. We must show that we understand their world so that they will be comfortable sharing their world with us.

It is not easy for most of us to be comfortable in our Grandchildren's world. We are all more rooted in the past than we realize or is good for us. We tend to be contemptuous of much that is new. We keep making comparisons with the "good old days". What our Grandchildren hear us saying is that we are worlds apart; different from each other. This is not the way to promote togetherness. We should revitalize our curiosity and openmindedness. Look at today with more flexibility and recognize that many things are better now.

Our goal is to be a very special grown up friend to our Grandchildren. Many of us have difficulty with the concept that our Grandchildren are our friends. We fear that this leads to spoiling them, and that we will reinforce bad habits and lose their respect. Grandchildren are well aware that we are not their Fathers; it is the Grandfathers who don't know how to stop being Fathers. We destroy our role if we become authoritative, demanding and punitive.

WHAT'S IN THIS FOR THE GRANDCHILD ?

Grandfathers help their Grandchildren understand and become comfortable with a world which can be pretty confusing. With the kind of understanding that only experience can bring, Grandfathers teach Grandchildren many important things, not the least of which are the simple skills (see Chapter 5) that make life interesting.

The history that we Grandfathers share with our Grandchildren comes from a generation which has seen and lived through more change than any in previous history. We provide a framework of family roots and continuity to foster a sense of place for our Grandchild. In addition, we help provide a set of values, strengths and beliefs that our Grandchildren must have to survive in this increasingly complex world.

Our Grandchildren learn from us what it means to be an elder. If we have a positive attitude about aging, our Grandchildren will be more likely to be optimistic about their own life. If we have a good relationship with our Grandchildren, they will transfer their affection for us to all adults. Hopefully, we add a sense of humor which may be missing in their other contacts with adults.

We demonstrate our commitment to their future success by supporting our Grandchildren and their parents in achieving a happy home life and providing a safety net when problems occur. No matter what happens, we assure them that we will still be their Grandfather and will always love them.

But most important of all, we add fun and excitement to our lives and create a optimistic approach to the future for both ourself and our Grandchild.

CHAPTER 3

The Rest of the Cast

ISN'T THIS REALLY A GRANDMOTHER THING?

Grandmothers have always had a major role to play in families. Historically, they not only have been there for the good times but have been there for the Parents and the Grandchildren in times of trouble. Grandmothers are known for their nurturing role, a role of caring for children, known as the "maternal instinct". Modern times and traditions have modified the Grandmother's role.

As family units have become separated by distance and women's options have grown, many Grandmothers are now in the work force.

After years of childraising, many middle aged women are finding satisfaction in the business world. There is little future for Grandmothers who hang around with nothing on their mind but Grandmothering. In other words, Grandmothers today operate in many worlds and are not just limited to the traditional family roles. Grandmotherhood is an enhancement rather than an exclusive way of life.

Males have historically been discouraged from a major nurturing role in the family. Fathers of several generations ago were not expected to be actively involved in the raising of children. Certainly Grandfathers were not to take any active nurturing role. Many Grandfathers still associate affectionate behavior with women. They shy away from hugs and kisses with their Grandchildren.

Today Fathers, either by choice or by necessity, are playing a major role in the nurturing of their children. Some Mothers and Fathers look at this as equality. Many Fathers relish the opportunity to get involved with the nurturing role and are doing an outstanding job.

Many Grandfathers prefer to let Grandmother take the dominant role with the Grandchildren, following along at best. We hold back from making a contribution to the lives of our Grandchildren. Grandmothers should not have to nudge us into a stronger role. It is not their responsibility to tell us or show us our role. We should take our place as an equal to Grandmothers with opportunities to lead, follow, correct, instruct, laugh and be serious with our Grandchildren.

If we don't, we are hurting ourselves by missing out on so much fun and satisfaction. We are short-changing our Grandchildren from the benefits of really knowing us as individuals and gaining from our experience and wisdom. We deserve the opportunity to have our life enhanced by Grandfatherhood just like the Grandmothers.

WHAT DO YOU MEAN I'M NOT IN CHARGE?

Okay, we're convinced we want to be active Grandfathers. Let's get to it, right? Wrong, we must first pass inspection. But who is going to inspect us, we're the Grandfathers! The answer, of course, is the Parents, our child and their spouse. Depending on their opinion of whether we will be a positive influence on their family's lives, they can either encourage or discourage our relationship with our Grandchildren. Legally, the Parents of our Grandchildren have all the rights and we have none.

Although most of us get along with our adult-children and their spouses, stresses still occur. The most important feature of a good relationship is to respect their right to a separate identity and adult status. Historically Mother-In-Laws have had some difficulty dealing with the loss of control over their children and we should support them with understanding as they deal with this issue.

There is no reason we can't develop a good relationship with the person our child loves enough to marry and the person who will be one of our Grandchildren's Parents. Our in-law children do not have to win our favor, they can be friends with us or not as they choose. If we want to be friends with them, it is we who must make the effort. We should approach the relationship as one of a younger equal.

There is no guarantee of success. The differences in values may be too great or the chemistry of personalities too incompatible. We should never place ourselves in the position of losing our own child and consequently our Grandchildren as well. If we cannot be friends with our in-law child, we need not

become enemies. Friendliness is still possible even if
friendship is not. It is up to us to keep the doors
open. When we turn critical toward our child's
spouse, where do we imagine our child's loyalty will
be fixed; certainly not on us.

At least a mention should also be made of the
other set of Grandparents, the parents of our child's
spouse. Under ideal circumstances, the two sets of
Grandparents would become friends; cooperating to
support a successful future for the Parents and the
Grandchildren. Unfortunately this is not the most
probable scenario. Usually the relationship ends up
being an on and off rivalry to win the most affection from our Grandchildren. As Grandfathers, we
should do our best to maintain cordiality in the
relationship and enjoy the time we do get to spend
with our Grandchildren.

WHAT'S IN THIS FOR THE PARENTS?

Grandfathers never escape from their most
important role in life, that of being a Father. As
Fathers, we have a history with our adult children
and that history is rarely one of total bliss. Many of
us have had it up to here with parenting especially
those of us that have been subjected to "parent

bashing" by our adult children. Others of us may be keenly aware that we made significant mistakes as Fathers. We may find it uncomfortable revisiting this history with the Parents of our Grandchildren. All of us have wounds and we can let them fester and fester over our entire lives if we don't take steps to heal them.

Our adult children, for the most part, really crave a good relationship with their parents. Many Grandfathers are successful in achieving good ties with their children's families and become a significant participant in their Grandchildren's lives. Grandfatherhood offers an opportunity for us to repair some of the damage that may remain from those days when our Children were seeking their independence and defying and denouncing us as reasonable Fathers. In some cases, maybe we weren't reasonable. However it is amazing, now that our Children are faced with raising their own offspring, how much more credit they will give us for our attempts at providing guidance to them when they were young. Our role now involves not only Grandfathering but also a bit of Parenting in the form of offering support and help.

As we pursue Grandfatherhood, our families, which many of us may have believed were seriously flawed, may start to function well again. Our

Children are reaching true adulthood. We have gathered our energy and are ready to focus on family concerns as well as our own individual pursuits. We can now share their Parenthood as a common bond.

Our Grandchildren have many needs. The best solution would be for their Parents to have the time and the resources to meet these needs. Unfortunately, many Parents are not delivering. Studies have shown that Parents are spending 40% less time with their children than they were as recently as 10 years ago. The Parents and the Grandchildren need both Grandmothers and Grandfathers to step in and help fill these needs. Grandparents may have been put on the shelf in the past but everyone now realizes that we are potentially one of the major players in solving the stress and problems that are developing in today's families.

What our adult child wants from us are the following:
- respect for their adult status and acceptance of their right to have their own viewpoints
- understanding, encouragement and a belief in their abilities
- open communications with them and advice when they ask for it
- understanding and acceptance of their spouse

- openly expressed love for them
- love, interest, and help with the Grandchildren
- freely given support when we can afford it
- our attempt to be as self sufficient and
  independent as possible
- acceptance of their help if needed

Obviously as a Grandfather we have not only the joys but many responsibilities thrust upon us. We are clearly needed. If we are successful in balancing and prioritizing these needs with the rest of the work and play that make up our life, then we will achieve tremendous satisfaction in knowing that this phase of our life has been so fruitful.

CHAPTER 4

Making the Connection

WHY CAN'T I JUST WAIT FOR THEM TO GROW UP?

Many Grandfathers have a tendency to postpone any real interaction with their Grandchildren until they reach school age. We rationalize this based on the male's traditional role of not being involved with the care of infants. In some cases, we are employed full time and feel we do not have enough time. We may also believe that there is little Grandfathering we can do with a young child.

Supposedly Grandparents are free to enter or leave a Grandchild's life at any time. Why not enter when Grandchildren can take care of themselves and then exit when the going gets sticky during adolescence?

On the surface, looking at it from the Grandfather's point of view, this approach is very appealing. Although there is no research data, this is probably the primary approach that Grandfathers have taken during the last 50 years. To really understand the impact of this approach to Grandfatherhood, we need to look at the effects on the Grandchild, the Parents, as well as the Grandfather. All children know that they are Grandchildren. If we do not become involved with our Grandchild, we are a figurehead Grandfather. They know that we exist but they do not know us. To know a Grandchild and to have a Grandchild know us we need to spend time together.

If we neglect the early years of our Grandchildren they have every reason to wonder whether we are really committed to this relation-ship. "Who is this person that waltzes in and waltzes out depending on his personal whims? Is he a fair weather friend or a trusted advisor?" Our Grandchildren will attempt to get to know us regardless of when we enter their life. But time does move quickly. The truth is that much of our

Grandfatherhood role can best be accomplished during those wide-eyed days of early childhood.

To be successful as a Grandfather, we need the help of the Parents. The Parents control access. They will either encourage or discourage the relationship we seek to develop with our Grandchild. One of the roles of Grandfathers is to provide support to the Parents and to share with them the common bond of Parenthood.

The raising of young children has always been a trying task. Today it is even more difficult for our children. If we provide support and a positive attitude, we will earn their respect. In return, they will be more likely to support our efforts with our Grandchildren. We can not expect them to single-handedly raise the Grandchildren without our interest and involvement and then welcome us with open arms when we decide, at our convenience, to enter our Grandchild's life.

A Grandfather can have fun with a Grandchild at any age. Postponing this fun till the child is older is precious time wasted and never regained. Building a loving relationship takes time. Not all of our Grandchildren may be responsive to us initially. The longer we work at Grandfatherhood, the better chance we have at being successful. Just like everything else, time and effort count.

WHAT DO YOU MEAN I SHOULD KEEP MY MOUTH SHUT?

Grandfathers have to walk a fine line when it comes to talking to both the Parents as well as the Grandchildren. In family matters, we are all guilty of too much talking and too little listening. What makes us unique to our Grandchildren is that we are usually the only adults that will take the time to listen to them.

When talking to our Grandchildren, we should ask questions that are interesting to them. Show we understand what they are saying. Our Grandchildren should be encouraged to be open and honest about their feelings and problems with us. Try not to be judgmental, just be their sounding board. Remember that people of every age are helped more by what they say than by what others say to them.

When our Grandchildren do ask our opinion, they will be much more likely to listen. Unlike their Parents, we are not "on their case" on a daily basis. We are less apt, hopefully, to nag them repeatedly about their deficiencies. We should go out of our way to provide a verbal "pat on the back" whenever it is justified. The more we praise and reward, the more praiseworthy things they will attempt.

Don't confuse a need to love and listen with permissiveness. Letting Grandchildren be undisciplined, selfish, or rude will only hurt them in the future. With respect to discipline, it is much easier for the Grandfather than it is for the Parent. We can exercise control by withdrawing our attention and our rewards. Rewards are privileges not rights. If they don't behave properly, withdraw the rewards and attention and look for an opportunity to start fresh at a later time.

The cardinal rule for a Grandfather is to never give advice to the Parents of our Grandchildren on anything unless we are asked. Based on our experience as a Father, we have come to many conclusions about raising children. We may be saddened to see our own Children make mistakes that could be avoided. The possibility of having us be considered an interfering Grandparent is totally unacceptable. We need to let the Parents find their own way. Hopefully they will seek our advice. Then, among a series of compliments, tactfully slip in any constructive criticisms. Most Parents today consider us insufficiently informed about modern parenting. In this area, the best way to proceed might be to consider ourselves as "Middle East Peace Negotiators" walking through a mine field without a detector.

DO I REALLY WANT A VISIT?

There are five types of visits between a Grandchild and his Grandfather:

- visit at the Grandchild's Home with the parents at home
- visit at the Grandfather's Home with the parents
- visit at Grandchild's Home with the parents gone
- visit at Grandfather's Home without parents
- visit during a day trip or vacation.

Visits are the basic building blocks in developing a relationship between Grandfather and Grandchild. To know a child and have them know us, we need to spend time together at frequent intervals.

Historically, the distance between homes was small. It was not unusual for a family visit to take place every few days or every week. Remember those ritual Sunday dinners? Most of us do not live this close to each other or do not choose to follow this routine any longer. While it was a convenient way to build a relationship, the weekly visit is not a necessity.

Family visits can be fun and useful but they do not make the total connection. Most of us love our Children and they love us. But getting together full time in the same house for several days with the Grandchildren can lead to many problems. What are these problems? How about too much adult talking, forgetting about the children, differences with living methods and habits, unsolicited criticism or advice, different house rules, differences in permissiveness with the children, and taking over cherished tasks versus being helpful.

Many times, when it is time to separate, we all feel not only relief but sadness that the precious time together was not as harmonious as we had hoped. Today about 50% of these family visits that require overnight travel result in a hotel or motel stay. One night in each other's home can be fun. If it's much longer than that, many of us prefer our own space.

In terms of accomplishing our role as a Grandfather, we will make little progress until we spend time with our Grandchildren without the Parents. One successful solution is to stay with the Grandchildren while the Parents take a much needed break. This can easily be a weekend for those of

us who are still working during the week. We get to
know the Grandkids and they get to experience us.
Many times it will create less disruption for the
Children if this Grandsitting is done at the Child's
home. It can be a real treat for us to see our
Grandchildren live their life instead of being parad-
ed by their parents. This is also a great time to
meet their friends; to really understand the environment that our Grandchildren are growing up in
each day. This will give us hundreds of ideas to talk
about when we are not able to be with them personally.

The key to getting Grandfather mileage from
this kind of visit is to make the time together special; make it fun for both of us. Loosen the rules a
little bit for the sake of the kids, take some day
trips or excursions, play with the kids, teach them
something (See Part 2 of this Handbook).

If the Grandchild or Grandchildren are coming to
our home, do some basic childproofing. If the child is
young, make sure there is nothing dangerous left
out. If there are prized possessions, put them away
instead of nagging at the Grandchild to keep away.
Sit them down and tell them the few basic house
rules which must be followed. Create a special
space for them and make them feel welcome and
loved. Follow the activities laid out in Chapter 6.

Make sure that they help with the everyday routines around the house. Try to find something special they are attracted to about the neighborhood, a pet, or a friend so we can talk and write to them about it when we are not together. As they get older, we should consider having them bring one of their friends along for the visit.

The most memorable times for our Grandchildren as well as for Grandfathers are when we have visits without Siblings or Parents. During these visits, we can truly discover each other as persons. We need only do those things that are special to both of us.

ISN'T GIVING MONEY EASIER?

Giving should be fun; fun for Grandfather to select and fun for the Grandchild to receive. Do not try to buy love with gifts; it won't work. Give gifts that demonstrate you understand what will delight this particular Grandchild. For birthdays have the Grandchild prepare a wish list and go over it with Parents. Birthdays are special to Grandchildren because it is their special day and birthday presents demand special attention. Depending on the childs age and attitudes, gifts of our time, such as a trip or outing, may be more valuable than a material gift.

Books are always appropriate. Identify a series that matches up with their interests. Check with librarians and children's bookstore personnel for an appropriate choice. A magazine subscription, suitable for their age and in their interest area, with their name on it will show our love during the year. Gifts should yield instant gratification; no bank accounts, stock, or coin sets. As Grandchildren get older, clothing can be a desired gift but it must be exactly what's in style and what they want. There is nothing wrong with a little selfish interest on our part in our gift giving. If we want to encourage an activity, give some equipment for activities like scouting, music, and sports. Maybe even a computer modem and software (see Chapter 10) that will enable us to communicate with fun and frequency.

Money is not a satisfactory gift by itself. If given with a small personalized gift and with a stipulation that it be used in a designated way (like a gift certificate for a particular type of store) it can work, especially for the older Grandchild.

The nicest gifts are the unexpected ones. A Valentine flower for our Granddaughter or a fancy dinner out for just the two of us. A set of ballgame tickets for our Grandson, his buddy, and Grandpa. A gift of theater or movie tickets that our Grandchild can give to their Parents will show them how much fun giving can be. These gifts stand out and are special; just as we are special Grandfathers with very special Grandchildren.

PART TWO

Having Fun Together

CHAPTER 5

Teaching a Grandchild

WHAT SKILLS DO I REALLY HAVE?

Nothing is more basic to the Grandfather/Grandchild relationship than the sharing of common activities. Nothing will bring about greater memories and real contributions to our Grandchildren than teaching them about an area where we have a particular skill. All of us have skills and hobbies that we enjoy. We need to determine which of these areas, that interest us, would also be of interest to each of our Grandchildren.

When we have the opportunity to be with our Grandchildren, we will then have the opportunity to explore these special shared areas together. During those times when we are not with our Grandchildren in person, these shared activities can be the basis for letters, telephone calls and gifts. The identification of these shared interests is one of the keys to a truly meaningful relationship.

Listed on the following pages are a number of areas where we and our Grandchild might have common interests. It is important that we identify areas where we have skills, interest and experience. Each of our Grandchildren should also identify some areas where they have a particular interest. Should the interests of our Grandchild and our skills and experience coincide, then we have an interest we can share together. If we find our Grandchild's interests lie in an area where we do not have a particular skill but it does sound interesting, then possibly it is an area where we could learn together.

MAJOR COMPETITIVE SPORTS

- BASEBALL
- BASKETBALL
- FOOTBALL

- HOCKEY
- SOCCER
- SWIMMING
- TENNIS
- TRACK AND FIELD
- VOLLEYBALL
- WATER POLO

PHYSICAL SKILLS

- ARCHERY
- BADMINTON
- BILLIARDS/POOL
- BODY BUILDING
- BOWLING
- BOXING
- DIVING
- FENCING
- GOLF
- GYMNASTICS
- HORSESHOES
- ICE SKATING
- ROLLER SKATING
- PING PONG
- SAILING
- SKEET/TARGET SHOOTING
- SKIING

- SHUFFLEBOARD
- SURFING
- WATERSKIING
- WRESTLING

OUTDOOR ACTIVITIES

- AUTO RACING
- AVIATION
- BACKPACKING
- CAMPING
- CYCLING
- DRAG RACING
- FISHING
- HIKING
- HORSEBACK RIDING/RODEO
- HUNTING
- MOTORCYCLE RACING
- MOUNTAIN BIKING
- OFF ROAD VEHICLING
- RIVER RAFTING
- ROCK CLIMBING
- SCUBA/DIVING
- TREASURE HUNTING

ANIMALS/PETS

- ANIMAL HUSBANDRY
- AQUARIUMS/FISH AS PETS
- BIRDWATCHING
- BIRDS AS PETS
- CATS AS PETS
- CAT SHOWING
- DOGS AS PETS
- DOG SHOWING
- HORSE SHOWING
- OTHER PETS

PLANTS/GARDEN

- BONSAI
- FLOWER ARRANGING
- FLOWER GROWING
- HERB GARDENING
- HYDROPONICS
- INDOOR PLANTS
- LANDSCAPING
- VEGETABLE GROWING

HEALTH/APPEARANCE

- AEROBICS
- DIET/NUTRITION
- GROOMING
- GYM EXERCISE
- WALKING/JOGGING
- WEIGHT TRAINING

FOOD PREPARATION/COOKING

- BAKING
- BBQ/SMOKING
- CAKE DECORATING
- CANNING
- CATERING/ PARTY PLANNING
- COUPON CLIPPING/ SHOPPING
- DEHYDRATING
- ETHNIC COOKING
- FREEZING
- LABEL READING
- LITE COOKING
- MICROWAVE COOKING
- VEGETARIAN

WORKING WITH HANDS

- AIRCRAFT MODELS
- AUTO REPAIR
- BIRD HOUSES
- CANDLE MAKING
- CAR MODELS
- CARPENTRY
- CERAMICS
- DOLL MAKING
- DOLL HOUSES
- ELECTRICAL
- ELECTRONICS
- EMBROIDERY
- JEWELRY MAKING
- KITE BUILDING
- KNITTING
- LEATHERCRAFT
- MASONRY
- METAL WORKING
- MINIATURES
- PLUMBING
- RESTORING VINTAGE AUTOS
- ROCKET MODELS
- ROBOT CONSTRUCTION
- SEWING
- SHIP MODELS

- STAINED GLASS
- WEAVING
- WOOD CARVING/WORKING

HOBBIES

- ANTIQUES
- ASTRONOMY
- ASTROLOGY
- COIN COLLECTING
- GUN COLLECTING
- HAM RADIO
- INDIAN LORE
- KNIFE COLLECTING
- MODEL TRAINS
- ROCK COLLECTING
- SLOT CAR RACING
- SPORT CARD COLLECTING
- STAMP COLLECTING
- WEATHER

ARTS AND ENTERTAINMENT

- ARCHITECTURAL DESIGN
- BALLET
- BALLROOM DANCING
- CLOTHING DESIGN
- COMEDY
- DRAMA
- INTERACTIVE VIDEO
- JUGGLING
- LINE DANCING
- MAGIC
- MUSIC COMPOSITION
- MODERN DANCING
- MOVIE MAKING
- MUSICAL INSTRUMENTS
- OIL PAINTING
- PENCIL SKETCHES
- PHOTOGRAPHY
- SCULPTURE
- SQUARE DANCING
- TAP DANCING
- TRAVEL
- VENTRILOQUISM
- WATERCOLOR

WORKING WITH THE MIND

- BRIDGE/ OTHER CARD GAMES
- CHESS/ OTHER BOARD GAMES
- COMPUTER PROGRAMMING
- DEBATE/PUBLIC SPEAKING
- INVESTING
- LITERATURE/READING
- WRITING

CAN'T I JUST SEND THEM TO A CLASS?

Many Grandchildren will have difficulty in iden-tifying their interests. It will be necessary to expose them to a particular hobby or skill to see if they show an aptitude or interest. A little bit of conver-sation and exploring with each Grandchild should yield at least one shared interest.

Ideally, we should select shared interests where the Grandchild has no other learning opportunities. For example, if our Grandchild has a Father who is able to teach sports and a Mother who is a wonder-ful artist, then it would be wise for the Grandfather to identify a shared interest in an area where the Grandchild has no teaching resource.

A Grandchild will have many capabilities and interests where neither the Parents or the Grandparents have skills, experience or interest. Grandfathers can support their Grandchildren and Parents by considering paying for outside instruc-tion. Obviously, this has to be done with the full agreement of the Parents. For the older Grandchild, suggest that the Grandchild provide, through their own work efforts, a significant portion of the funds that are required. We all know that when it involves someone's own labor, there is a much higher poten-

tial that the Grandchild will be a serious participant. It's a great values lesson as well as an opportunity to learn another skill.

Of course, professional instruction is available in
all areas. Why not just buy the kid the best possible
instruction in everything and forget all the extra
effort to get the Grandfather involved? The missing
ingredient is the time spent together getting to
know each other. The teaching of the skills is a tool,
the final product is the memories.

CHAPTER 6

Grandchild Activities

HOW CAN I KEEP THIS CHILD BUSY AROUND THE HOUSE?

When we get the opportunity to be with our Grandchild or Grandchildren, that is when the FUN begins. Time together will include visits with us at our house, visits when we take care of them at their house, and trips and outings. The more planning that we do for this time together, the more successful we will be as a Grandfather, and the more FUN it will be for both of us. Grandfathers must recognize that children have limited attention spans and high energy levels.

If our time together is to be fruitful and fun for
both of us, we must have a program for our time.
Many of us think a Grandchild visit means an
outing to an amusement park. While that may be
enjoyable, there are many other activity choices to
consider. As a start, try turning off the television set
except for very special situations. If we were just
babysitters, we would leave the TV on but we are
Grandfathers.

The very best activities can be the simplest such
as doing household chores together. Share our jobs
with the Grandchildren. Let them help wash the car,
rake the leaves, shovel the snow, and get the mail.
Of course it will take longer since they do not have
adult skills, but it is a wonderful opportunity to
talk together. When we need to go out to the mar-
ket or the hardware store, take them with us. Use
the experience to find out what they like and know.
Teach them about something they don't know or
understand.

Stockpile a few things to fix when they come to
visit. We should teach our Grandchildren, boys and
girls, about common tools and their safe use. Give
them something to take apart. If we take care of
them at their house, we should look for a bike or
toy that needs a little work. Teach them to maintain their own things.

Remember that parents today spend 40% less time with their children than 10 years ago. Since they have such limited time with their children, many of the shared activities and skills that we took for granted, as parents, simply do not exist in today's family routine.

No where is this more likely to be evident than in the kitchen. Resist the temptation to take them out to a fast food restaurant. They probably have a lot of experience doing that. Get them, both girls and boys, involved with planning, shopping, setting the table, helping fix and serve, and doing the dishes as appropriate to their age level. Make it FUN for both Grandfather and Grandchild by not trying fancy stuff. Let them learn how to safely do simple things like muffin pizzas and making cookies.

During our time together we will get a chance to work with them on our common interest activities and hobbies. We can also find something new that both of us would like to learn about. Also try to find an activity where the Grandchild can teach the Grandfather something new like a card game, a playground activity, or as a last resort a video game. Keep that TV off in the evening by playing games, reading books, and going over picture albums.

WHERE CAN WE GO THAT WILL BE INTERESTING?

Outdoor activities and day trips are the real specialty of Grandfathers. For the younger Grandchild, these will take the form of wagon rides and walks around the block and visits to the local playgrounds. As they get older, we should pack a lunch and their trike or bike, a kite and a ball and take them on a picnic at a park. Better yet do an outdoor cookout.

A list of out-of-home activities and day trips includes:

- the most important out-of-home visit that a Grandfather and Grandchild can take is a visit to the library. When children learn to love reading, their education and future become noticeably brighter.
- visit zoos, aquariums, children's museums, gardens and observatories. Tour factories, airports, fire stations and hospitals. Attend naval ship open houses, airshows, rodeos and country fairs.
- arrange a visit to the places where family and friends work

- visit the seashore or a lake or river. Swimming, tidepooling, boating, sailing and fishing if there is a good chance to catch something.
- visit the mountains or countryside. Take a hike. Learn how to read a map and compass. Identify birds, flowers, plants and bugs. Take along a camera that the Grandchild can operate and maybe a sketch pad.
- take the Grandchild to a performance such as a children's theater, an ice show, or a circus. Take in a film documentary at the regional IMAX theater.
- As the Grandchild matures, consider high school, college and professional sports, light opera, and a play or ballet.
- activities we can do together like horseback riding, tennis, batting cages, miniature golf, bowling, golf lessons, the golf driving range, shooting instruction and firing ranges. For the adventurous take a one-day train trip, or a ride on a hot-air balloon, a glider, or a small plane. There are one day white water raft trips and deep sea fishing trips.
- accompany us on whatever community volunteer activities that we perform.

CHAPTER 7

Traveling with a Grandchild

WHY RUIN A GREAT TRIP BY BRINGING A GRANDCHILD?

Grandfathers are the most ardent travelers of all. We travel more often, farther and for longer periods of time than anyone else. Traveling with a Grandchild, under the right circumstances, can make a trip even that much better. What better way to have our Grandchild one-on-one for some quality period of time than a trip together. So what if our travel sidekick is a half a century younger.

We must take a few steps to ensure the experience will be fun for both of us such as:

- picking a destination and an itinerary that will be fun and interesting for both the Grandfather and Grandchild.
- not making the trip too long. About one week is maximum for a child and two weeks for a teen. Try to be part of a group where there will be some other children the same age as our Grandchild. This can give us both a break from each other occasionally.
- try to incorporate a form of travel that the Grandchild has not experienced before; an air plane flight, a train trip, a horseback ride, or a cruise ship voyage.

Most of us will plan our own trips. We should get our Grandchild involved in the planning process. Go to the auto club together and get maps and to the library to get information on things to see. If possible, go to the travel agency together to make reservations. If we aren't close enough to do this together, maybe the parents can help with getting the child involved in researching the trip. We can talk by phone about what information we have both found.

Trips we might consider could include the following:

- locations and events that are being studied in school by the Grandchildren such as Revolutionary War Battle Sites, Washington D.C., Missions, etc.
- visits to conventions or regional exhibitions that are tied into the common interests that we share with our Grandchildren. National Championships of a particular sport, a Cat or Dog Show, a Coin Collectors Convention, are examples.
- outdoor camping and backpacking adventures and visits to scenic wonders like our National and State Parks, Forests and Monuments.
- urban experiences like New York, Chicago, and San Francisco

Grandfathers have found that taking a Grandchild on a trip is one of the best possible ways they can get to really know each other while having FUN.

CAN'T WE GET SOME HELP PLANNING THIS TRIP?

As a result of the popularity of these types of trips, many organizations are now sponsoring trips specifically planned for Grandparents and Grandchildren including:

- **ELDERHOSTEL** - if over 55, this well known educational travel organization has a number of trips designed to give both Grandfather and Grandchild a good time while we enjoy one another's company unhassled by everyday pressures. (617)426-8056
- **FAMILYHOSTEL** - an international travel and learning program for families in the summer. (800)733-9753
- **GENERATIONS** - a tour service exclusively for Grandparents and our Grandchildren which aims to make this type of travel fun and worry-free and to strengthen Grandchild/Grandparent bonds. (312)404-2400
- **GRANDEXPLORERS** -designed to help Jewish grandparents pass on their heritage and values to Grandchildren. (202)857-6577

- **RASCALS IN PARADISE** - a family tour service that invites Grandparents and Grandchildren along. (800)872-7225
- **GRANDTRAVEL**- first agency to offer special trips for Grandparents and their Grandchildren so they can share the pleasures of traveling together. Their 1995 catalog offers eight domestic tours from Alaska to New England and nine international tours to such locations as Australia, Kenya, Israel and Europe. (800)247-7651
- **AMERICAN WILDERNESS EXPERIENCE**- specializes in backcountry adventures for Grandparents and Grandchildren including wagon train trips, river rafting, and snowmobile adventures. All year round. (800)444-0099
- **LUXURY ADVENTURE SAFARIS** - exclusive safari specifically for a Grandchild and their Grandparent. (805)967-1712
- **R.F.D. TRAVEL** - schedules a couple of trips each summer like cattle drives, or wagon train trips for Grandparents and Grandchildren. (800)365-5359
- **VISTATOURS** - bus tours of United States specifically for Grandparents and Grandchildren. (800)248-4782

- **WARREN RIVER EXPEDITIONS**- offers a Grandparents/Grandkids raft trip down Idaho's Salmon River every summer. (800)765-0421
- **AMERICAN MUSEUM OF NATURAL HISTORY**- runs family educational tours and welcomes Grandparents. (800)462-8687

Also the Cruise lines have some outstanding short inexpensive cruises that are ideal for a great trip with a Grandchild. The staff on these cruises really go all out to make the Grandchildren feel special. Many of these cruises have on board a special staff person who runs a Junior Cruiser program for the kids. This gives Grandfather a break. The meals, transportation, shipboard activities, and shore tours are all packaged. With proper selection, this can be the perfect Grandchild trip. These are only a few of the group travel programs specifically designed for Grandfathers to have quality time with our Grandchildren.

WHERE CAN WE GO THAT WON'T COST A FORTUNE?

Some of the best times for the least expense might be a campsite or cabin near the seashore, a lake or a stream. What better one on one experience could there be than this type of trip?

If our travels require a hotel room or an airline ticket, their are many discounts available for people over 50. There is an entire book devoted to these discounts entitled, "Unbelievably Good Deals & Great Adventures That You Absolutely Can't Get Unless You're Over 50".

For the Grandfather who really is searching for a creative way to strengthen the ties with his Grandchildren, try a trip together. Our Grandchild is much more interested in our interest and our time than in the amount of marble in a hotel lobby. Our Grandchild is much more interested in experiencing a sunrise over the Grand Canyon than in a twenty-five dollar Sunday Brunch. A Grandfather/Grandchild trip is an exciting fun activity which will create unforgettable memories.

CHAPTER 8

Family Ties

WASN'T "BACK TO THE FUTURE" A MOVIE?

Grandchildren need to look to their future with hope. One of the best ways to achieve hope is by sharing our family history with them. Learning their family's past gives them a connection to the world and the confidence to better face their future. In other words, the ability to look back strengthens their prospects for a bright future. It is Grandfather's role to provide this continuity between the past, present and future for our Grandchildren.

There are a number of ways to communicate the history of our family to a Grandchild. Each Grandfather will be comfortable using his own technique. There are no incorrect methods. The end result is to transmit to the Grandchild the strength and continuity of the family and to translate these roots into an optimistic view of our Grandchild's future. One of the tools that we can use is the family photo album.

Family photos have a way of finding their way into a disorganized box or boxes. They do little for the child in that form. There are photo albums designed specifically for a Grandfather to compile a family history. One album, "Grandfather Remembers", has places for a complete family tree of photos as well as a number of open end questions that we are to answer. These questions discuss the how's and whys of our life with Grandmother, our career, the birth and life of our Grandchild's Parent and the birth of our Grandchild. In addition there are questions regarding the things that we remember about the world such as current events, music and books. Completing a book like this is a wonderful first tool for our task of communicating our family memoirs.

There are other photo related tools that a Grandfather should prepare. The first is a detailed picture album of our Grandchild's Parent. Grandchildren love to look at pictures of their own Parents when they were young. It gives them confidence when they see their now responsible Parent was once a child just as they are a child.

Put together this Parent photo history in chronological order. Put in pictures of their homes, their friends, their birthday parties, their cars, their pets, their vacations and their participation in sports, hobbies, and school activities. Make this Parent's Book special for each Parent and only deal with pictures and captions describing them.

These books make wonderful Christmas presents for a Grandfather to give to his own Children. Not only will Parent Photo Album's please the Parents but they are wonderful tools for the Grandfather to use with the Grandchild. In fact this will probably be the albums primary use. Our Grandchild will see his Parent, as a child, growing up in a happy, healthy, family environment. This will enhance their desire to bond with the family. They will see the security and fun that family ties are able to provide to children. For the same reason, it will also enhance Grandfather's standing with the Grandchild as the person who made all these wonderful times possible for their Parent.

Another great family photo tool that Grandfather can prepare is a set of picture collages that can be hung on the wall for easy access by the Grandchild. These can take the form of a series of large framed posters each titled around a family tree heading. For example:

- "Planting the Roots" would consist of picture groupings dealing with the early days of Grandfather's family (wedding, early house and auto, births of children and infant photographs)
- "Watering and Feeding" would cover the years of Grandfather's family when the children were growing up. Picture groupings would center around each child in the family as they grew up. Show their activities family trips, and pets.
- "Branching Out" introduces dating and marriages of the children and the Grandchild sees the introduction of both their parents, and their marriage. Also shown is the emergence of aunts and uncles as adults and Grandfather and Grandmother in middle age pursuits.
- "New Growth" illustrates the Grandchildren joining the family. Other areas will show the growth of the tree as the Grandchild's Aunts and Uncles have their families and cousins appear.

It is possible to continue to add several more posters as the family matures. The idea is to tie the various families and Grandchildren together into a giant, strong, spreading family tree. Each Grandchild can see that they are an important part of this tree. Inevitably, each Grandchild will be drawn to these pictures on their visits. As the years go by the questions will flow. When a new poster goes up, each will crowd around to first see their own growth and then the growth of the rest of their family tree. Grandfather meanwhile will be able to enjoy this panorama of his family and can take great pride in showing it off to his friends.

Many Grandfathers take reviewing the family photo albums to another level by using them as props for family story telling. As the Grandchild grows, Grandfather should introduce, now and then, a discussion of events and relationships that may not have been all that wonderful. All families have problems along the way and it is important for our Grandchildren to recognize that mistakes do happen and that life does have its' disappointments. We need to develop their tolerance of human individuality. Possibly we can use these albums to illustrate and help them understand what they may be going through with their own parents.

One of the most powerful tools that Grandfather can utilize in communicating the family history is the creation of the family video. Using his own voice, stories, and pictures, Grandfather, with a Camcorder, can develop this video. What a wonderful gift for his Grandchild. What a treasure for the Grandchild to be able to hear Grandfather's own words thirty or forty years later as he recounts his own experiences as a youth, as a husband, as a father, and as a Grandfather.

SINCE WHEN ARE THE "OLD DAYS" BORING?

Most Grandfathers like to talk about memories, When we talk to our Grandchild, sometimes we drift into comments about how easy people have it today, or how lousy many things are today compared to when we were growing up. Nothing will turn off a Grandchild faster than a Grandfather who continually faces backward and degrades the Grandchild's world. They must have dreams of a better tomorrow; a tomorrow that they will help create for their future.

We must be able to achieve a proper balance of yesterday and tomorrow in our conversations or we will lose the respect of our Grandchild. Nostalgia is great, but if given as a steady diet, our Grandchild may consider us unimportant in their lives and future or just plain boring.

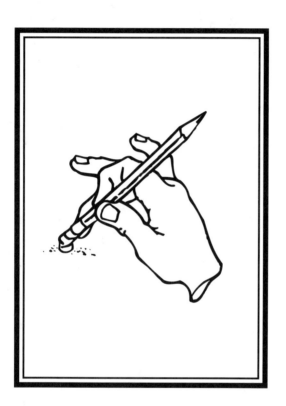

CHAPTER 9

Planning for Success

ISN'T BUILDING A GRANDFATHER PLAN A LITTLE TOO MUCH?

Being a special Grandfather seldom just happens. We need to create opportunities to share time with our Grandchild. We need to make the most of this time. We need to add flair to the activities so our Grandchild will know that they are special in our eyes. If we do not chose to be a mediocre Grandfather, we need a plan to achieve these goals. Planning will identify opportunities for both the Grandfather and Grandchild.

A successful Grandfather Plan will put into practice the ideas that have been presented in this handbook that are pertinent to our situation . It is impossible to achieve success as a Grandfather overnight. No one, especially our Grandchildren, will be waiting around for us to announce that we have become interested in being a Grandfather this month.

Good Grandparenting happens step by step over time. Some suggestions on preparing useful tools for becoming a successful Grandfather are as follows:

- A good place to start is with the inventory of our skills and expertise as outlined in Chapter 5. Try to identify an expertise or a desire on our part to learn a skill in each of the areas. For example, if we have no skills in the area of plants/garden but have always had an interest in learning hydroponics, check it under interest. We don't have to be world class experts to check a skill. Just make sure that it is something we really enjoy. It makes little sense in trying to get involved in something with our Grandchild where we ourselves have no real interest. Our Grandchild will pick up our lack of interest immediately. It's got to be fun for us too.

- depending on the age of the Grandchild, it may
be possible to start introducing them to some
of these skills now while others will have to
wait for a more appropriate age.
- try to get the Grandchild's Parents to help us
with matching up our skills and intcrests with
a Grandchild's interests. It won't be perfect but
over time we will be able to identify at least
one area where we and each of our
Grandchildren will have a shared interest. This
does not have to be an earth shattering activity to enable both of us to enjoy special times
together.
- assemble a Grandparent Notebook with a section for each Grandchild. Enter in key facts
about each Grandchild such as the name of
schools, teachers, special friends, team names,
scores, schedules, favorite hero's, favorite foods,
etc. presents given and received, places visited,
books read, and interest areas they may have
talked about with us before. This set of notes
should help us have great phone conversations
that actually get above the pleasantries all
children think are boring. It will also key us
to areas where we can clip articles of interest
that can be sent to them including suggestions
for future presents, joint activities and trips.

- start compiling the information on family ties that was outlined in Chapter 8 such as:

  1. albums on each Parent growing up
  2. Family Tree collages for the wall
  3. "Grandfather Remembers" type book/video

Tools can be a great help but only if we spend adequate time with our Grandchild. We need an annual plan (see an example on the following pages) that will ensure that:

- we have communication with each Grandchild (Parents don't count) once every two weeks.
  - personal visits
  - telephone conversations
  - mail (electronic or written)
  - tape (video or audio)
  - see Chapter 10 for ideas
- we have at least 6 personal visits a year with each Grandchild (Visits to Parents don't count unless we spend at least an hour with the Grandchild alone.)

- we do at least 3 activities out of the home a year with our Grandchild as suggested in Chapter 6.

- we have an annual project together with our Grandchild in our special shared area. We should share our achievements annually with the rest of the family over the Holiday period if possible.
- when our Grandchild becomes old enough, we should enjoy a trip together at least every two years.

This is not a work assignment, it is a roadmap to Fun. It can only be fun if it is a natural result of our wanting to build a long-term bond with our Grandchild. If we are just going through the motions without making the effort to understand each other then we should both skip it.

SAMPLE GRANDFATHER PLAN

BETWEEN: Grandfather (YOU) & Each Grandchild

GRANDFATHER\GRANDCHILD
SPECIAL SHARED ACTIVITIES
　　i.e. BASEBALL, CAMPING OR ANY OF OTHERS
　　FROM CHAPTER 6

COMMUNICATIONS
　　IDENTIFY SPECIFIC THINGS THINGS YOU AND
　　YOUR GRANDCHILD WILL DO DURING THE
　　YEAR TO COMMUNICATE,
　　　　i.e. GRANDCHILD WILL CALL YOU ABOUT
　　　　RESULTS OF HIS OR HER BASEBALL GAMES,
　　　　YOU WILL SEND INFORMATION ON POTEN-
　　　　TIAL CAMPING TRIPS

VISITS
　　PRELIMINARY PLAN FOR GETTING TOGETHER
　　THIS YEAR,
　　　　i.e., GRANDPA TO ATTEND IN PERSON AT
　　　　LEAST TWO BASEBALL GAMES, GRAND-
　　　　CHILD TO VISIT GRANDPA OVERNIGHT WITH
　　　　BEST FRIEND

ACTIVITIES

SOME IDEAS FOR THINGS TO DO TOGETHER
THIS YEAR,

> *i.e. SEE A PRO BASEBALL GAME TOGETHER*

PROJECT

MAKE A COLLECTION OF ROCKS THAT WE
FIND ON OUR CAMPING TRIP

LAST YEAR

GRANDFATHER'S BEST

THE BEST THING THAT HAPPENED WITH
YOUR GRANDCHILD,

> *i.e. WHEN YOU CALLED ME ABOUT YOUR*
> *REPORT CARD*

GRANDCHILD'S BEST

THE BEST THING THAT HAPPENED WITH
YOUR GRANDFATHER,

> *i.e. WHEN YOU BOUGHT ME A NEW BASE-*
> *BALL GLOVE FOR MY*
> *BIRTHDAY*

THIS YEAR

GRANDFATHER HOPES

SOMETHING YOU WANT TO IMPROVE WITH
YOUR GRANDCHILD,

*i.e. YOU WILL STAY OVERNIGHT AT
GRANDPA'S HOUSE*

GRANDCHILD HOPES

SOMETHING YOUR GRANDCHILD WANTS FROM
YOU,

*i.e. DON'T HUG ME AFTER THE BASEBALL
GAMES*

PARENTS

GRANDFATHER HOPES

SOMETHING THEY CAN DO TO HELP YOU GET
CLOSER WITH YOUR GRANDCHILD,

*i.e. SEND ME A COPY OF THEIR BASEBALL
SCHEDULE*

PARENTS HOPE

SOMETHING THEY WANT YOU TO DO THAT
WILL HELP THEM WITH THE GRANDCHILD,

*i.e. DON'T MAKE PROMISES ABOUT A CAMP-
ING TRIP AND THEN NOT DO IT*

WHAT DO YOU MEAN I COULD BE A BETTER GRANDFATHER?

So we think we can all be perfect Grandfathers if we accomplish all the tasks and milestones that were discussed earlier. Wrong, we will always have areas where we can improve. The real question is whether we wish to identify these deficiencies and make the effort to improve.

There are a number of ways to identify areas where improvement is needed. First, we can analyze our performance ourselves. Second, we can ask our Grandchild. Finally, the "Rest of the Cast", outlined in Chapter 3 is usually more than willing to indicate our deficiencies (real and imagined). In an ideal situation, we would seek input from all three sources.

A self-examination is relatively painless and can be quite useful if we give it a fair shot. We can easily evaluate our performance in terms of effort by matching, on an annual basis, time spent versus time planned. We should keep in mind that these numbers are not based on any study results, they are just set at a level that will challenge us and will meet the needs of many relationships. If we are retired and live down the street or we work full time in a distant land, we may be able to do more or less than the guidelines suggest. If our Grandchild is an infant we should attempt more face to face visits. Grandfathering is never the same. Situations change continually. We have a responsibility to recognize and seize every opportunity for a meaningful relationship with each Grandchild.

While we can get a handle on the effort we are making, the actual quality of the time we spend together is a totally different matter. Certainly we know whether we are having fun together which is a primary indicator that things are working well. We might ask our Grandchild to sit down with us each year and help us with next year's Grandfather Plan. This is a great time for both of us to discuss things that may be bothering both of us like:

- respect for each other and our individual differences
- equality of treatment
- personal traits that bother each of us

Obviously a 5 year old Grandchild is not going to interact in the same way as a rebellious teenager.

The teenager will probably not even communicate with us unless we have taken the trouble to communicate with them during earlier years.

In a similar fashion, we should also sit down with the Parents (hopefully two) of the Grandchild each year with our Grandfather Plan. We should certainly get their inputs on our relationship with their child and how it might be improved. In addition, we must also candidly discuss how well we are performing our continuing role as Parent. Chapter 3 provided a list of what our adult child expects of us. If we are not meeting their expectations, we should know about it and discuss it. None of us wish to make our Children unhappy and we certainly want to do everything possible to make them satisfied with our performance as a Grandfather.

As we have previously discussed, Parents can put a kink in our relationship to our Grandchild. We must use great caution in discussing problem areas with our adult children and their spouses. If anger and resentment sets in, we will probably be the loser regardless of the right and wrong of it. If they suggest changes we should be open to discussing them. Offer no advice unless asked. If we truly have problem areas, they should be discussed and not swept under the rug. The annual review of the Grandparent Plan is an opportunity to get problems discussed in the natural course of events without creating a crisis situation. We should try to use it this way.

We should not be hesitant or embarrassed about asking our Grandchildren and their Parents to help us with our Grandfather Plan. There are no rules about what has to be in such a plan or that it has to be written. Our Grandchild truly wants a Grandfather and will respect that we are making the effort and that we care enough to include them. Parents know that they need all the help they can get. If we are smart enough to ask for their advice and keep our "cool", the annual Grandfather Plan discussion can open up all kinds of wonderful doors.

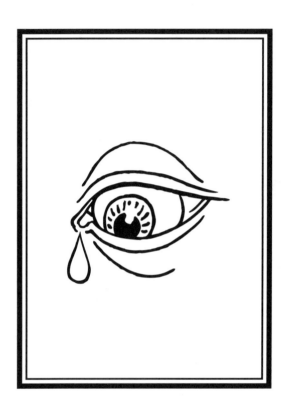

PART THREE

Dealing with Problems

CHAPTER 10

We Live too Far Away

WHAT CAN THIS CHILD AND I TALK ABOUT ON THE PHONE?

It was great to do all those wonderful activities with our Grandchildren. What can we Grandfathers do to keep our relationship with our Grandchildren strong when we are not together? Telephone contact helps fill this need. Most of us know, from our experience as Fathers, that it is not easy to get children to talk freely in person much less over the telephone.

Some Grandchildren are reserved and some just don't like the pressure of a lot of questions from an adult. Children like to keep personal business to themselves because Parents and teachers are always correcting them. Our Grandchildren learn very fast that since their answers to questions don't measure up with adults, maybe they should just keep quiet.

Grandfathers inherit this problem and we must try and find a way around it. One of the easiest problems to avoid is trying to communicate when the Grandchild is hungry. We should try and call our Grandchild's family after mealtime. It makes good sense to time our calls when the family is not involved in preparing and eating their meals. We are not going to be a hero if we call right when the spaghetti water is boiling over. After a meal, hopefully, our call will be well received by the family and our Grandchild will be relaxed with a full tummy.

To achieve good communications with our Grandchild we must be indirect, subtle and gentle. The basis of our conversation should be those special things that we know about each other. We need to know what they like to do and think. Before our call, we should review our Grandchild's Notebook, see Chapter 9. We should try to get them talking about their favorite things in life, their activities, and their friends. Remember the success of those business calls where we asked our bosses and clients about their wives and children by name and knew each of their hobbies. The same holds true of our Grandchild calls. Hopefully we will have identified a few things that have happened since we last talked to them. For example, if our Grandchild is interested in baseball then we start out, "How about those Dodgers, isn't that three wins in a row"?

The real challenge about telephone conversations with our Grandchildren is to get them comfortable with calling us. We want them to feel like they can pick up the phone and talk to us about their problems and their accomplishments. Somehow we need to get them to take that first step of calling us, their special friend. Using the same analogy of baseball, we could jointly manage a fantasy league baseball team together. Each Sunday morning our Grandchild could read the box scores and then call us so we could talk about what moves we should make. It doesn't have to be sports, it could be a game we are playing, a special television program we could discuss, laugh lines, or even recipes from the food section. We just must get them over the hurdle of calling us. If they feel uncomfortable doing this as a child, we will have lost them by the time they are teenagers.

One answer might be to have them contact us by computer using an on-line service. The challenge and excitement of technology might help break down communication barriers.

CAN'T WE JUST SEND GREETING CARDS?

While telephone calls are considered the next best thing to a personal visit, the smaller child, of two or three, may get more from a package, or a picture postcard. Grandfathers don't have to be professional writers to create an interesting post card.

Here are a few handy hints about communicating by mail with a Grandchild:

- Always address whatever we send to the Grandchild. Our young Grandchildren receive very little mail and it is really special for them to get a piece with only their name on it.
- Collect postcards that have pictures that are unique to the interests of each Grandchild.
- Make what ever we send distinctive. Use stickers or put in a special surprise in every envelope.
- When they are starting to read and write, we should get them their own special writing sup-

plies and stationary and envelopes with their names printed. Maybe even funny return address labels.

- We should put up a bulletin board where all the correspondence and drawings from our Grandchildren are posted. Make sure they know, either by a picture or during a visit, that we are proud of everything they send us and want all our friends to see their work.

- Try to include a photo or a picture with everything you send. Pictures usually create more interest than just words.

It is important that our Grandchild develop a vision of what we look like. We should send them a photograph. Sometimes a frame mounted photo is not compatible with being placed in the Grandchild's room. One easy solution for the Grandchild in school is the Calendar. Take a piece of cardboard and at the top mount a good sized snapshot of Grandfather and Grandchild doing something together. Make the bottom a monthly calendar page that we can take off a throw-away calendar. Mount the month on a sheet of paper that also has a special picture of something our Grandchild really likes (jet planes, pets, flowers, football players, etc.). Now we have something we can send to each

Grandchild each month for them to mount on their calendar. Hopefully they will check the calendar regularly and there will be our joint picture.

Packages are great and very special. Send little inexpensive things throughout the year. A small reading book from a series our Grandchild likes. Clippings of events or things where the Grandchild has expressed an interest. Pins, jacket patches, decals, seed packets, photos, calendar pages, fastfood gift certificates, puzzles, coloring albums, jokes, comic books, small toys, recipes, harmonica, magnet; the list is endless.

Put something in each package that they have to complete and send back to us like a word puzzle. Encourage them to send you copies of their school work after it comes down from the refrigerator door as well as a schedule of their games and meets. Include a self-addressed stamped envelope.

WHAT THE HECK IS THE INFORMATION SUPERHIGHWAY?

So what kind of communication is left after we have discussed telephone calls and the mail? Welcome to the new world of multi-media and cyberspace, our Grandchild's world. The definition of the Information Superhighway is just being written. The only thing we really know for sure is that within the next 5 years, there will be an explosion of new exciting ways for Grandfather to communicate with his Grandchild.

The next edition of this handbook will probably be published in electronic form. Letters are fast being replaced by E-Mail and Faxes. Equipment for making and playing videos is widely available in American homes. We see family get togethers taking place using video conferencing techniques. Without a home computer, a Grandchild is at a disadvantage. Why our own new Speaker of the House is going to get many of us out of a cycle of poverty by having the Government provide us with a lap-top computer.

Your Grandchild lives everyday with Nintendo and Sega. Grandfathers must develop the will to keep up with the times if we are to successfully communicate with our Grandchildren. We need a much broader perspective of today's life than is provided by our own peer group. We need to take into account the values, goals, skills, and concerns of our Grandchildren as well as their Parents if we want to keep off the shelf.

A good place to start might be to join Senior Net, a non-profit organization, (415) 750-5030, for people over 55 that helps members learn about computer and communications technologies. Senior Net has learning centers around the world and their own on-line network. With a telephone line, modem, and SeniorNet Online software, we can join thousands of members sharing information on a wide range of topics. We can begin to use this technology to communicate with our Grandchild.

Let us resolve that one of our trips with our Grandchild will be a ride down the Information Superway together. We will be quite surprised to see how this new generation can drive this highway. We might even find that we will be having the time of our life using our flight simulation program. On Sundays, we could find ourselves having "aerial dogfights" with our Grandchildren who may be thousands of miles away from us. It sure beats doing the crossword puzzle.

CHAPTER 11

Ups and Downs

WHY CAN'T EVERYBODY JUST GET ALONG?

The Rand Corporation, a well known

research institute in Santa Monica, California has

compiled the results of 200 recent research studies

of the children of American. Their conclusion; "It's

harder than ever to be a kid today". How, in a

Country that is so economically and militarily

strong, can this be happening to our grandchildren?

We live in a Country where the middle ground, by almost any factor that we measure, that was prevalent in the 1960s is disappearing. This leaves more children growing up in either have or have-not homes. These have-not homes are primarily headed by women. The number of these women headed families has tripled since 1960. Fatherless families have increased to account for a quarter of all American families. One in two of our Grandchildren will grow up in a home where the Father is absent for six years or more.

The causes include a divorce rate that has tripled since 1960 to 60% and an out-of-wedlock birth rate of over 25% which is 5 times higher than the 1960 figure. Only half of our Grandkids that come from divorced families saw their Dad last year. Only one in three of these divorced Dads sent their full child-support payments.

According to William Bennett, former Secretary of Education, the results are showing up in our Grandchildren. In 1940, when many of us started school, teachers identified the top problems in America's schools as: talking out of turn, chewing gum, making noise and running in the hall. In 1990, teachers listed drugs, alcohol, pregnancy, suicide, rape and assault. Yes, it is harder than ever to be a kid.

Even in our two-parent families, the average parent spends just seven hours a week with their children, a third of the time we spent with our children in 1960. Reports of child abuse and neglect are also up sharply in the last decade.

The hard fact is that these changes were not something done to us and our families: they are changes we have done to ourselves. There is a coarseness and a cynicism to our relationship with our institutions and our communities. The worst of it has to do with our Grandchildren. Our culture seems dedicated to their destruction as moral human beings.

Our interest has waned in many key areas. According to George Will, since 1973 the number of Americans who report having attended a public meeting in the past year has declined from 22% to 13%. Participation in parent-teacher associations has declined from 12 million in 1964 to 7 million today. As a Country, we have forgotten the importance of our Children and Grandchildren. Not only are we not getting along, we don't even seem to care.

DO I REALLY NEED TO GET INVOLVED?

Grandfathers offer many reasons to avoid becoming involved with their families and Grandchildren. Some of us reject the Grandfathering role because we associate it with old age. Some of us feel that we have no authority and do not want to butt in. Some of us have no familiarity with the role because we had no exposure to our own Grandfathers. Some of us feel uncomfortable with any role which involves raising children. Some of us are embarrassed because we recognize that we did a poor job in raising our adult children.

Some of us have been rejected by our Grandchildren or by our Grandchildren's Parents. Some of us will not make the effort needed to overcome the distance we live from our Grandchildren. Some of us have found other options to Grandfathering and we just don't want to put up with the hassle of being involved with our families.

Many of us are divorced and some of us are remarried and find the complications and uncomfortableness of blended families too hard to overcome. An increasing amount of us find that, with the rise in divorces among our adult children, we are shut off from even seeing our Grandchildren.

When our Grandchildren turn out to have physical or emotional problems, some of us just don't want to deal with them. Some of us have rejected our own adult children because of drugs, differences with their spouse or any number of other reasons. If we want to find a reason to be uninvolved, it is clear that all of us can find a reason.

So it all boils down to the answers that have been provided in this handbook. Chapters 1, 2 and 3 provided a summary of "what's in it" for the Grandfather, Grandchild, and Parents. It is in our best interest, selfish as that may be, to become involved with our Grandchildren even if we have to overcome a lot of these obstacles along the way.

Will being a great Grandfather help solve some of the bigger picture problems of our family structure, communities, and Country? Can one more great Grandfather make a difference? Of course it can and it is.

Grandparents are now the primary Parents of their Grandchildren in 5% of our nation's households; that is real sacrifice. While there is sometimes little that we can do to save a marriage, we can make sure that the Children of that marriage are protected. As a group, Grandparents control over 60% of the financial assets of this Country and we spend 20 Billion Dollars a year on our

Grandchildren. We are a huge voting block and we exercise our voting rights. Now that the Baby Boomer Generation is about to join us, Grandparents will become even stronger. YES, WE CAN MAKE A BIG DIFFERENCE.

WHY DON'T I CALL IN A PROFESSIONAL?

Perfection was never one of our strongpoints when we were Fathers. We will not be perfect Grandfathers either. Our Grandchildren can handle a certain amount of imperfection and most thrive. There are limits to the problems that a Child or Grandchild can handle. Learning disabilities affect an estimated six million of our Grandchildren. Physical disabilities affect many millions more. Millions of our Grandchildren are in homes where there are serious problems such as drugs, alcohol, mental illness, child abuse, and spousal battering. Even Grandfathers can have these kinds of problems. Many of our Grandchildren have problems with drugs, sexual promiscuity, and violence themselves.

Few of us are experts in these fields. We are incapable of solving these types of problems without professional help. Stop condemning our families and get them some help. We should seek help for ourselves if we need it. If we can not control our own problems, we are only adding more stress on our families.

A list of Professional Organizations which can provide Assistance is included in the Appendix of this handbook. It is a place to start, there are thousands more.

To get the attention of our Governments, we should consider supporting the recently proposed "Contract With America's Children". This contract is sponsored by the Coalition for America's Children, a bipartisan umbrella group of 300 organizations that serve children like the Junior League, the United Way and the National PTA .

TEN PRINCIPLES OF THE CONTRACT WITH AMERICA'S CHILDREN

CHILDREN FIRST - We promise to consider children's needs and well-being, first and foremost, in evaluating health and welfare reforms, or any other national policy.

HEALTHY CHILDREN - We promise to ensure that children get the basics they need to grow up healthy.

CAPABLE CHILDREN - We promise all children the chance to realize their potential, and we expect all parents to join in this promise by becoming active partners in their child's education.

SAFE CHILDREN - We promise to reduce the exposure of children to violence -on television, on our streets and in our homes -and to educate the public about the risks of firearms.

FAMILIES TOGETHER - We promise to support marriage, help families stay together and help young people understand the responsibility of parenting.

WORKING FAMILIES - We promise to help working families stay out of poverty.

FAIR CHANCE - We promise to support a family's efforts to get ahead by making sure that continuing education and training are available to people of all means.

VALUE YOUTH - We promise to provide young people with places to go and things to do that will help them become responsible members of our society.

COMMUNITY RESPONSIBILITY - We promise to do our part in our own community to support all children's healthy development.

LEADERSHIP ACCOUNTABILITY - We promise to hold our elected leaders accountable for their responsibilities to safeguard the future of America's children.

Source: The Washington Post

EPILOGUE

GRANDPA, WHY ISN'T EVERYBODY HAVING THIS MUCH FUN?

It is easy to lose out on the joys of being a Grandfather. If we undertake Grandfatherhood with the idea that we will be rewarded if we do a Grandfather Plan and we religiously follow all the recommendations, we may miss the entire point. Stand back from your Grandchildren and observe them as they develop. As Fathers, we were much too close. The details of everyday living did not permit us to detach ourselves. We can't help but be proud that we had a role in making these little lives possible. We can not help loving them, not because they call us or write us, but because they are simply wonderful unique human beings. OUR REWARD IS A PASSPORT WE RECEIVE FROM THEM. A passport to participate, with them, as they grow and mature into worthwhile adults.

To make Grandfatherhood FUN rather than work, we need to enter into their childhood with a sense of adventure and discovery. If we have a spirit of play, they will respond with a spirit of play. If we are comfortable being with them, they will become comfortable with us. They will accept us for ourselves. If we show sensitivity, understanding, discretion and kindness they will respond in time. If we treat our Grandfatherhood as a wonderful privilege rather than another duty, we will be well on our way to making this FUN. Then perhaps your Grandchild, too, will run up one day and say, "GRANDPA, THIS IS FUN".

APPENDIX

GRANDFATHER RESOURCES

ALCOHOLISM

Al-Anon including Alateen,

Box 862, Midtown Sta. New York, NY 10018

(800) 356-9996

ANOREXIA NERVOSA/BULIMIA

American Anorexia/Bulimia Assoc.

418 E 76th St., New York, NY 10021

(212) 734-1114

BIRTH DEFECTS

March of Dimes Birth Defects Foundation,

1275 Mamaroneck Ave., White Plains, NY 10650

(914) 428-7100

BLINDNESS

National Society to Prevent Blindness,

500 E. Remington Rd., Schaumburg, IL 60173

(708) 843-2020

CANCER

Candlelighters Childhood Cancer Foundation,

7910 Woodmont Ave., Ste. 460, Bethesda, MD 20814

(800) 366-2223

CHILD ABUSE

Parents Anonymous,

520 Lafayette Park Pl., Ste. 316, Los Angeles, CA

90057. (800) 421-0353

CYSTIC FIBROSIS

Cystic Fibrosis Foundation,

6931 Arlington Rd., #200, Bethesda, MD 20814

(800) 344-4823

DIABETES

Juvenile Diabetes Foundation International,

432 Park Avc., New York, NY 10016-8013

(800) JDF-CURE

DISABILITIES

National Easter Seal Society,

70 E. Lake St.., Chicago, IL 60601

(312) 726-6200

National Information Center for Children and

Youth with Disabilities

Box 1492, Washington, DC 20013

(800) 999-5599

DRUG ABUSE

National Families in Action

2296 Henderson Mill Road, Ste. 300, Atlanta, GA

30345. (404) 934-6364

EPILEPSY

Epilepsy Foundation of America

4351 Garden City Drive, Landover, MD 20785

(301) 459-3700

HEARING AND SPEECH

Alexander Graham Bell Association for the Deaf,

3417 Volta Place N.W. Washington, DC 20007

(202) 337-5220

National Association of the Deaf-Blind

814 Thayer Ave., Silver Spring, MD 20910,

(301) 587-1788

National Association for Hearing and Speech

Action, 10801 Rockville Pike, Rockville, MD 20852

(800) 638-8255

National Stuttering Project,

2151 Irving St., #208, San Francisco, CA, 94122-1609

(415) 566-5324

LEARNING DISABILITIES

Learning Disabilities Association of America

4156 Library Rd., Pittsburgh, PA 15234

(412) 341-1515

MENTAL RETARDATION

National Down Syndrome Congress,

1800 Depster St., ParkRidge, IL 60068-1146

(800) 232-NDSC

The ARC

500 E. Border St., Ste. 300, Arlington, TX, 76010

(817) 261-6003

MULTIPLE SCLEROSIS

National Multiple Sclerosis Society,

733 3rd Ave., New York, NY 10017

(800) 624-8236

OBESITY

Overeaters Anonymous,

383 VanNess Ave., Ste. 1601., Torrance, CA 90501

(800) 743-8703

ORGANIZATIONS FOR YOUNG PEOPLE

American Red Cross, National Headquarters,

431 18th St. NW, Washington, DC 20006

(202) 737-8300

Big Brothers/Big Sisters,

230 N 13th St., Philadelphia, PA 19107

(215) 567-7000

Boys & Girls Clubs of America

771 1st Ave., New York, NY 10017

(212) 351-5900

OSTEOGENESIS IMPERFECTA

Osteogenis Imperfecta Foundation

5005 W Laurel Ave., Ste. 210, Tampa, FL 33607-3836

(813) 282-1161

SUDDEN INFANT DEATH SYNDROME

SIDS Alliance

10500 Little Patuxent Pkwy, Ste. 420, Columbia, MD

21044. (800) 221-SIDS

BIBLIOGRAPHY

BOOKS

Aldrich, Robert A., and Glenn Austin. "Grandparenting for the Nineties". Escondido, Calif.: Erdmann Publishing, 1991.

Bowman, Norman H., Sallie Jagger Hayes and George Newman. "The Grandparenting Book:101 Tips and Ideas on Enjoying Life with Your Grandchildren". Blossom Valley Press

Carter, Lanie. "Congratulations, You're Going to be a Grandmother: A Guide to Helping the New Family". Oak Tree Publications,

Dalton, Rosemary. "Encyclopedia of Grandparenting". Bristol Publications,

Dodson, Dr. Fitzhugh, and Paula Reuben. "How To Grandparent." Harper/Lippincott

Elkind, David. "Grandparenting, Understanding Today's Children". Glenview Ill.: Scott Foresman and Co., 1990

Endicott, Irene. "Grandparenting Redefined". Lynnwood, Wash.: Aglow Publications, 1992

Fromme, Dr. Allan. "60+: Planning It, Living It, Loving It" Farrar, Straus and Giroux Inc.

Goode, Ruth. "A Book for Grandmothers". McGraw-Hill

Heilman, Joan Rattner, "Unbelievably Good Deals & Great Adventures That You Absolutely Can't Get Unless You're Over 50". Chicago, Ill.: Contemporary Books, 1994

Kornhaber, Dr. Arthur, with Sondra Forsyth. "Grandparent Power". New York, N.Y.: Crown Publishers, Inc., 1994

Kornhaber, Dr. Arthur, and Kenneth L. Woodward. "Grandparents/Grandchildren: The Vital Connection". Doubleday

Krueger, Caryl Waller. "The Ten Commandments for Grandparents: A Wise and Witty Handbook for Today's Grandmas and Grandpa's". Nashville, Tenn: Abingdon Press, 1991

LeShan, Eda. "Grandparents: A Special Kind of Love". MacMillan

Madden, Myron C. and Mary Ben Madden, "For Grandparents: Wonders and Worries". Westminister Press

Shedd, Dr. Charlie W. "Then God Created Grandparents and It Was Very Good". Doubleday

Slaybaugh, Charles S. "The Grandparents' Catalog". Doubleday

Strom, Robert and Shirley Strom. "Becoming a Better Grandparent". Thousand Oaks, Calif.: Sage Publication, Inc.1991

Wasserman, Selma. "The Long Distance Grandmother". Port Roberts, Wash.: Harley and Marks, Inc., 1988

White, Linda B. "The Grandparent Book: Thoroughly Modern Grandparenting". San Francisco, Calif.: Gateway Books, 1990

INDEX

INDEX

Ordering Information

Telephone Orders: (909)-337-0914
Have your VISA or MASTERCARD ready.

Postal orders: Great Times Press
P.O. Box 378
Lake Arrowhead, California 92352

Copies of Grandfather's Handbook are $12.95 each. Plus sales tax of $1.00 each (7.75%) for orders shipped to California addresses.

Shipping: via US Mail
$2.00 for 1st book + $0.75 for each additional book.

If paying by credit card please provide the following information:
Credit Card (Visa, Mastercard),
Card number,
Name on Card,
Expiration Date,

Provide shipping address including,
Name,
Address,
City, State
Zip Code   and Telephone number